TEXAS

A Photographic Journey

TEXT: **Bill Harris**

CAPTIONS: **Pauline Graham**

DESIGNED BY: **Teddy Hartshorn**

EDITORIAL: **Gill Waugh and Pauline Graham**

PRODUCTION: **Ruth Arthur and David Proffit**

DIRECTOR OF PRODUCTION: **Gerald Hughes**

DIRECTOR OF PUBLISHING: **David Gibbon**

CLB 2455
© 1990 Colour Library Books Ltd., Godalming, Surrey, England.
All rights reserved.
This 1991 edition is published by Crescent Books,
distributed by Outlet Book Company, Inc., a Random House Company,
40 Engelhard Avenue, Avenel, New Jersey 07001.

Random House
New York • Toronto • London • Sydney • Auckland

Printed and bound in Malaysia

ISBN 0-517-01492-0

10 9 8 7 6 5 4 3

TEXAS

A Photographic Journey

Text by
BILL HARRIS

CRESCENT BOOKS
NEW YORK • AVENEL, NEW JERSEY

A giant fiberglass iguana on lower Fifth Avenue in New York City marks the location of a little home-away-from-home for Texans living in exile in the Big Apple. If the iguana is out of its element, a surprising number of Texans are not. Down home in the Lone Star State, more than eight out of ten of the people live in cities.

Houston covers more than 600 square miles, and is one of the most important cities in the United States. Dallas, the city that gave Texas "culture," and the rest of the country the Neiman-Marcus department store, calls itself a "Metroplex." And San Antonio, a city with a tradition both Easterners and Europeans can understand, has never stopped growing since before there was a place called Texas.

Though it was once an independent country, all Texans are Americans today. But most other Americans would agree they are a breed apart. The common stereotype is of big, loud men in white hats and high-heeled boots given to lots of whooping and hollering, lying and bragging. According to the myth, they drive big cars, drink hard whiskey, and if they're not millionaires, they surely will be soon

Most Americans react to that image in the same way they react to puns. But, like a good pun, even a Texan who fits the stereotype is a joy to behold. The fact is, though, it's only an image. There are more millionaires in Minnesota than there are in Texas, more big cars in Los Angeles, and you can buy high-heeled boots in San Francisco or a big, white hat in New York. Oh, sure they whoop and holler a bit. They have a lot of good things to shout about. And what sounds like bragging is often just simple statements of fact. As for lying, well, Walter Cronkite is a Texan, and he didn't get to be TV's top newscaster by telling fibs.

The common denominator in the Texas personality is probably found in the name itself. In the early 16th century, Spanish explorers moved north from Mexico in search of the fabled "Seven Cities of Gold." Moving east from Arizona and New Mexico, a group of explorers made contact with a tribe of Caddoan Indians living in the Texas Panhandle. They were unusually friendly, especially compared to the Apaches the Spaniards had already met. Impressed, the explorers described them with one of their own words, *Teychas*, which means "friend." In Spanish, the word took on a "j" sound and became *Tejas*. In written form, the "j" was an "x," and so, with the stroke of a pen, this friendly place in the Southwest became known as Texas.

If the natives were friendly, the Conquistadores were not. They stole the Indians' belongings and rode off into history. The original natives have long since gone and so have many of the types that replaced them. But the name still fits perfectly, because whatever else today's Texan may be, today's Texan is basically friendly.

Children in Texas learn the history of their own state before they find out about the rest of the country or the world. And that, more than anything else, may be why native Texans consider the world a dull place compared to Texas.

The Spanish, of course, did a lot more both for and to Texas than give it a name. Before they arrived, the Indian tribes in America had never seen a horse. They hunted buffalo and fought their wars on foot. Obviously, they were no match for the Spanish cavalry, which must have been as terrifying and as devastating as airplanes and tanks in World War I.

The horse they brought to Mexico was no ordinary horse. They called them mustangs. They had been introduced to Spain by the Moors, and were a cross between Arabian and North African breeds. They were bred in the desert, and were almost as good as camels when it came to getting along without water. The horse didn't need grain, preferring to feed on grass, and it seemed to thrive in the hot, dry climate of the Southwest. The mustang was small and fast; in a word, perfect for this new land. The land was perfect for the mustang, too, and they reproduced at an astonishing rate.

The Indians recognized a good thing when they saw it. Many of them worked as slaves for the Spaniards, and their duties included taking care of the horses. That gave them both a skill and a means of escape. Runaway slaves took mustangs out into the plains and up into the mountains, and completely changed the way their brothers lived.

It wasn't too long before the Apaches knew as much about horses as the Spanish did, and they used the knowledge to raid Spanish settlements to steal more horses. Having mustangs made it possible for the Indians on the plains to hold out for the next three centuries against the tide of civilization.

Word spread to the north about this wonderful gift of the white man and tribes from the Rocky Mountains wandered down into Texas to have a look and to steal some horses for themselves. Among them was a small tribe Indians everywhere called "enemy." When the Spanish met them, they agreed and gave them the Ute name for enemy, *Komantcia* – Comanche.

They had lived in the mountains, but they weren't farmers. They didn't have much taste for hunting buffalo on foot. But with a horse they could, and did, change their lives. In fact, they became the greatest horsemen the world had ever seen. They moved out onto the plains and spent the rest of their existence on the move. They followed the huge buffalo herds, and from the backs of their horses were able to kill as many of the beasts as often as they needed food, a warm robe, a new saddle. Their numbers grew along with their skill and their strength, and within a generation they began to cast greedy eyes on the territory to the south. The territory we call Texas.

They arrived in the 1720s armed with long lances and buffalo shields tough enough to stop a bullet. They could handle a bow and arrow better than any other tribe, and could avoid an enemy's arrows with a trick of riding parallel to the ground over the side of their horses. Genghis Khan himself might not have been a match for these warriors who struck by night, then vanished as if by magic.

Even the Apache, among the fiercest of all the native tribes on the North American continent, were no match for the Comanche hordes. Most of the Apache moved farther west, and those who remained in Texas were banished to the hills. The rich open hunting grounds became the undisputed property of the horse people.

At about the same time Benjamin Franklin moved down to Philadelphia, J.S. Bach moved to Leipzig and settlers from Massachusetts began expanding westward into Vermont, the "native" population of Texas became something different than it had ever been. Although European colonists would find hostile savages in all parts of North America, none would prove more hostile or more savage than the Plains Indians, who, in a way, were as much newcomers to Texas as the Europeans themselves.

A great many Apache stayed in Texas, to be sure, and thanks to the assault on their territory by their brothers from the North, they were angrier than ever. In almost any other terms, it would be reasonable to wonder why they couldn't come to terms. The land they fought over is vast. The distance from Brownsville, where the Rio Grande meets the

Gulf of Mexico, to Amarillo, up in the Panhandle, is just about the same as the distance from New York to Chicago. The Sabine River, the eastern border, is as far from El Paso to the west as the distance between London and Budapest. And if you were to cover a map of Europe with a map of Texas, you'd cover all of France, Belgium, the Netherlands, Switzerland and West Germany. You'd also cover Great Britain south of Manchester, Denmark south of Copenhagen, Italy north of Florence, half of Austria and most of East Germany.

Is it any wonder Texans are forced to use big words to describe their homeland?

When the Spanish first went into Texas, they took ideas from the old country that didn't fit. The Indians didn't see the advantages of the feudal European system and the land itself was too vast to tame with techniques that had been developed on the other side of the Atlantic.

But in Mexico, they were developing new techniques. Cortés had brought cattle to Mexico in the 16th century and over the next 200 years it became obvious that these tough, ugly longhorns were the key to the future. They were turned loose on the range and watched over by a new breed of mounted farmer called *vaqueros*. Because they were mounted, they were relatively free of the restrictions their brothers in Europe had to live with. They became independent and tough, though still tied to the *rancheros*, the owners of the cattle they herded and the huge estates they rode.

Their culture gave Texas some words that are common there to this day ... the place they worked was a *rancho*, they tamed *broncos* in their *corrals*, their buildings were covered with *adobe* and occasionally the sun would drive them *loco*. They themselves, *vaqueros*, gave latter-day cowboys the name *buckaroo*.

And just as they had given mustangs to the Indians, they gave longhorn cattle to the Southwest. At the time the Americans in the Northeast were fighting for their independence from England, Spain was well established in Mexico and seemed well on the way towards conquering the land to the north.

They had no idea of the fight they would have on their hands.

The Spanish never made any serious attempts to colonize Texas, and by 1820, when politicians in the United States began to take notice of it, there were less than 5,000 people living there and no one accused them of being Spanish. Except, that is, the Spanish themselves and officials up north who had just swapped it for five million dollars and the Florida peninsula. Some officials, of course, didn't think it was a good trade. Thomas Jefferson, for instance, at that time nearly eighty years old but still looking at the future of his country, wrote: "The Province of Texas will be the richest state in our union, without any exception."

But the deed had been done. Texas was a Spanish colony and anyone who lived there was a Spanish subject. Furthermore, they didn't have much use for *Anglos*. When the United States bought the Louisiana Territory from France in 1803, Texas was just across the border, and some Americans just naturally wandered over the line. But the Spanish gave them the bum's rush and made it clear that if you weren't willing to call yourself Spanish, you weren't welcome west of the Sabine.

On the other hand, some *Anglos* were willing to call themselves Spanish. After all, what's in a name when there's a fortune to be made? One of them was a Connecticut Yankee named Moses Austin. He had some experience as a Spanish subject when he moved his family west and opened a lead mine near St. Louis in 1798. At that time, St. Louis was part of Louisiana and Louisiana was part of Spain. Austin became a

Spanish subject and he became rich, too. And six years later, he became an American again after the Louisiana Purchase.

After the War of 1812, his fortunes began to slip and the great Depression of 1819 wiped him out completely. But Austin wasn't the sort to let outside events ruin his life. He had failed before. First in Philadelphia, then in Richmond. And each time he found opportunity by moving west. Besides, as he put it, "to remain in a country where I had enjoyed great wealth, in a state of poverty I could not submit to."

And so, a few days before Christmas in 1820, Moses Austin arrived in San Antonio to ask the Spanish Governor for permission to settle 300 American families in Texas. It seemed perfectly reasonable to him. After all, he was a former Spanish subject and you'd hardly notice 300 families in a territory as huge as this.

But the Spanish Governor didn't quite agree. He'd had trouble with *Anglos* before and didn't want any more. Jean Lafitte, the American pirate, was making trouble for Spanish ships from his base in Galveston. And, quite simply, the Governor felt it was his sacred duty to keep Texas free of all Americans.

"Being much disgusted and irritated by his reception," as Austin put it, he left the Governor in defeat. But as he crossed the plaza, he spotted a familiar face. It was another American who called himself Baron deBastrop. DeBastrop had been involved in adventures in Louisiana and had known Austin there. But when Louisiana became American, he kept his Spanish citizenship and moved west to San Antonio. DeBastrop had some influence in Spanish Texas and he had sympathy for Austin's plight. He convinced the Governor that this idea was too great to reject unilaterally and suggested that the problem be given over to his superiors in Mexico. The Governor agreed, and, to his surprise, so did his superiors. Austin's petition was approved in January, 1821.

Austin, meanwhile, went back to the United States to round up 300 families who would share his dream in Texas. But fate stepped in again. Within six months he had died of pneumonia.

His son, Stephen Austin, was meanwhile getting his first taste of failure at twenty-seven, trying to find a job in New Orleans. As the son of a rich man, he had the advantages of a private school education in New England, and had been to college. He had picked up good business experience and had learned the fine art of politics as a representative in the Missouri territorial legislature. He had served as a judge in Arkansas, and was studying law when his father convinced him he should join the great adventure in the West.

By the time he got there, of course, his father was dead and the job of establishing the American colony had fallen on his shoulders.

When Austin's delegation arrived in San Antonio, they were given a cordial welcome no American had ever seen in Texas. Events were going forward to declare Mexico independent of Spain, and part of that independence, apparently, was to put on a friendlier face. Things went smoothly for him, and it didn't take long for him to find a site for his new colony. He chose the lower valleys of the Brazos and Colorado Rivers and, once again following in his father's footsteps, headed back to the United States to find some people who wanted to move there.

His plan was to find people of "good character," and to offer them a section of land for the man of the family, one-half section for his wife and one-quarter for each of his children. If he had slaves, that entitled him to an extra eighty acres for each of them. In return, he proposed to charge twelve and a half cents an acre. Business was good at first, and by the beginning of 1822, some 150 men were at work clearing land for their new homes. But then the new government in Mexico stepped into the picture. They had a new policy on colonization, they said, and this idea simply wouldn't fit at all.

To straighten things out, Austin took a six-week, thousand-mile trip on horseback to Mexico City. When he got there, he wondered why he had gone to so much trouble. He said he was "... ignorant of the laws, the language, the forms, the disposition and feelings of the government." When he left there a year later, he was an expert in all those things. And that was a good thing for Texas.

When he went back to Texas, he had a new contract for his colony that was better than the one his father had negotiated. It allowed him to introduce the same 300 families his father had contracted for, but each family would be given 4,428 acres of grazing land and 177 acres of farm land. Austin himself would be given more than 100,000 acres.

The contract was completed in the spring of 1825 when 300 families had agreed to Austin's terms for settling in Texas. About twenty of the "families" were actually groups of single men who had joined together to take advantage of the generous land grants. By harvest time in 1825, these families, who are still known as the "Old Three Hundred," gave Anglo Texas a population of 1,800, including 443 slaves.

Austin's contract with Mexico made him head of the militia, with the rank of Lieutenant Colonel. It made him chief magistrate and legislator. It gave him the potential to become a dictator. But Stephen Austin didn't have the potential within him. In fact, under his influence, the city he built, San Felipe de Austin, thrived as the most important city in American Texas, and it didn't have a jail.

There was almost no crime in his colony, and he chose to deal outside the court system whenever he could. He wrote all the laws himself and, naturally, some colonists resented him. At one point they revolted over the twelve-and-a-half-cent-per-acre fee he charged, saying he was getting rich on their labors. To settle the argument, the fee was reduced. Money seems to have been the least of Austin's worries. He was the ultimate civilized man and his purpose in life, as he saw it, was to spread civilization. That was rewarding enough.

He was one of the most skillful politicians America has ever seen. He understood people perfectly and knew exactly how to deal with them whether they were Mexican Royalists or Republicans, Southern planters or rugged frontier farmers. He was honest almost to a fault, and sincere. He had no hidden motives, and that dumbfounded the politicians in Mexico, who had nothing but. His sole vision, as he put it, was to "redeem Texas from its wilderness state by means of the plow alone, in spreading over it North American population, enterprise and intelligence." He believed passionately in what Americans called "Manifest Destiny," a Divine call to destroy anything in the path of their civilization.

Austin never did quite fit the popular idea of a Western colonizer. He wasn't a "rough and ready guy." On the contrary, he was soft-spoken, well-dressed, well-mannered, polished. He found violence offensive and believed in the beauty of the law. He was single-minded about his project, and because he never found time for courtship, stayed single all his life. If anyone wanted to settle in his colony, they were guests in his house until they could find the right spot to build their own. If anyone needed money, he loaned it to them. If they needed an argument settled, he was the man they turned to.

Once the "Old Three Hundred" were settled and thriving, Austin got permission to expand the colony, and within a decade, 1,500 North

American families called themselves Texans. In that short time, they had brought more civilization, built more towns and cleared more land than the Spanish had in three centuries.

Their success encouraged more men to establish colonies like Austin's and Americans streamed west to fill them. But no one matched the success of the original. They did, however, lure great numbers of people into Texas, and within ten years, there were 20,000 North Americans putting their stamp on the wilderness, outnumbering the Mexicans by five to one.

To say they didn't get along with each other would be an understatement.

Just as the colonies in the North had been troublesome to their mother country, England, Texas, or more accurately, Anglo Texas, was a thorn in the side of Mexico. On the Mexican side, politicians and editorial writers were warning against this hostile menace. "We gave them land," they said, "we allowed them to live among us as neighbors. But their hearts are not with us. They want to take Texas from us, and we must be on our guard!" In many ways they were right. Though Mexico was a republic, its revolutions had never succeeded in giving power directly to the people as the American Revolution had done. The European minority kept control and kept the huge population of Indians and mestizos, or half-breeds, tied to the same old feudal system that was behind the revolts in the first place. The system stretched into Texas, and these new "Mexican" citizens with names like DeWitt, Robertson and Williams, didn't find it too comfortable.

The trouble came to a head in 1826 in Nacogdoches. A man named Hayden Edwards, following the example of Stephen Austin, had gotten a Mexican grant to settle 800 families in East Texas. But when he got there, he discovered that people were already living there, and though many of them had no legal papers to back up their claims, they clearly weren't interested in moving on. In the confusion, the Mexican Government cancelled his contract and told him to go back home to Kentucky.

No way, said Edwards. And he proclaimed a new republic, which he called "Fredonia," and dared the Mexicans to try to stop him. They did, of course, and most of the revolutionaries went back to the United States. But in the process, they fired the imagination of their fellow Americans, who always did love a good fight, especially when it's little guys against big guys. It made more Americans want to be part of the Texas adventure, and it made the Mexicans more determined to keep them out.

By that time, there were ten North Americans to every Mexican in Texas, and the Mexicans had been relegated to the lowest class. The Americans built schools, plowed land, cleared forests and seemed tireless in making the place their own. The writing was on the wall, and just about everyone in Mexico could read it clearly.

At the heart of it was ethnic hatred. Nineteenth-century Europeans, quite simply, didn't like each other. And the dislike, naturally, spilled over into the New World. The Anglo-Saxons didn't mind living among the Hispanics in the Southwest as long as there was no need for much eye to eye contact. But to protect its interests, Mexico introduced laws restricting immigration and forcing the Anglos to deal more directly with their superiors south of the Rio Grande. "Superiors." There was the rub.

The situation festered for several years, with an armed attack on a Mexican fort here; hurled insults at Mexican officials there; and general grumbling everywhere. Eventually, even Stephen Austin, who had spent eighteen months in a Mexican jail after an attempt to get the authorities to liberalize their attitude, was convinced the time had come for Texas to join the United States. He called out for stepped-up immigration; he clearly wanted any measures that would help the Anglo society in Texas survive and prosper.

The Mexican President, Antonio López de Santa Anna Pérez de Lebrón, who was a military leader of the first order, had his own ideas. He sent a large army across the Rio Grande toward San Antonio. When word of it reached Austin, he put out a message to all the Anglos in Texas: "War is our only resource. There is no other remedy."

Most of his followers agreed. But they didn't all agree with the idea of joining the United States, nor of fighting for independence. What they wanted, they felt, was to be left alone, and to stand up for their "rights." And to send that Mexican army back down south where it came from.

A few minor victories emboldened them, and soon a tiny army of 300 men under the command of Austin, who was now a General, was on its way to attack San Antonio. As they marched, they picked up more recruits, men who had come from places like Tennessee and Kentucky armed with the deadly long rifles that had conquered those lands a generation before. When they got there, the Mexican General had lost the advantage by not attacking first, and was forced to retreat into the town and allow it to be surrounded. Naturally, he sent for reinforcements from Mexico.

But in the meantime, what they had was a "Mexican standoff." Inside, the Mexican troops were starving and demoralized. Outside, the Texans, not able to attack because of lack of artillery, were getting hungry, too. And cold. Winter was coming, and not many of them had brought blankets or coats. Little by little, volunteers changed their minds and went home to their families. But enough stayed to keep the Mexicans bottled up.

And then something strange began to happen.

Word spread across the United States that something big was happening in Texas, and thousands with adventure in their souls wanted desperately to be part of it. In some places, they organized themselves into groups and set out for Texas. In many places, men simply dropped what they were doing, packed their belongings and headed west.

One such man had preceded them by a few years. He had arrived with good credentials, most important among them that he was a close personal friend of the President of the United States, Andrew Jackson. He was raised in Tennessee, and had, in fact, been its Governor. When his wife left him his political fortunes slid, and he drifted into Texas where he lived among the Cherokees. They called him "Big Drunk."

When the revolution broke out, he had already joined the cause and was serving it with distinction. Later he would be named Commander in Chief of the Army, and later still would become a United States Senator from Texas.

His name was Sam Houston.

If Houston had been born a hundred years later and decided to become an actor instead of a statesman, John Wayne would have been forced to film light comedies. He stood a good six foot three inches tall, though some said even taller. He weighed more than 240 pounds, all of it muscle, and he had long blond hair and steel-gray eyes. He clearly commanded respect. More important, he deserved it. "Honor" was the most important word in his vocabulary, and he exercised it in a way only a 19th-century man could understand.

He was a legend on the frontier, and the thrill of fighting by his side lured many from all over the South. And when they arrived, they became Texans to the core. Many of them died for the privilege.

By early December in 1835, the Texans outside San Antonio decided it was time to go inside, and a force of about 300 attacked. After five days of close hand-to-hand fighting, the Mexicans, a force of more than 1,100, surrendered. The Texans were in control of the fortress the Mexicans had named the Alamo.

They had also captured Goliad, and so controlled the two main forts on the San Antonio River that would protect them against attack from the south. It seemed that the war was over. They had stood up for their rights and made a good showing of it. There were no Mexican soldiers in Texas any more, and the Texan army began to disband and return to their farms. After all, Mexico was hundreds of miles away across the desert. They had captured enough cannon to protect the Gulf ports. The Texans weren't independent, of course, but they didn't care. They had asserted their right to be left alone.

But they hadn't taken Santa Anna into account.

The General who surrendered at the Alamo was the President's brother-in-law. And that made the defeat a personal thing. Within a month, he assembled a substantial army and set out for San Antonio. He reached Laredo in less than six weeks, and a short time later arrived within sight of the Alamo to the very great surprise of the defenders inside.

The Texans had raised a Mexican flag over the Alamo. They were, after all, citizens of Mexico. Over the flag they had lettered the numbers 1824 as a symbol that they were fighting for a return to the constitution in effect in that year, and not against the Mexican Republic. Santa Anna, meanwhile, in another act of symbolism, raised a blood-red flag as a signal to the defenders that he would give no quarter. And so, the Mexican Army fought under an alien flag in an attack on a fort that flew their own banner.

The Alamo on that day was under the command of Lieutenant Colonel Buck Travis, an officer in the regular Texan Army. His co-commander, Colonel James Bowie, had earned a reputation all over the frontier as an Indian fighter and a slave runner with the notorious pirate, Jean Lafitte. He was a known killer, having killed, among others, the son of Lafitte, who crossed him. But he was also a courtly gentleman who had moved as easily in the society of New Orleans as he did on the wild frontier. He fought with a knife his brother had made, and the knife became better known than he himself. He married the daughter of the Vice-Governor of Texas, and as a result owned huge tracts of land in the territory. When his wife and children died in an epidemic, he joined the revolution, became a friend of Sam Houston's and was sent to reinforce the garrison at San Antonio.

Not long after he arrived, thirteen more men armed with long rifles joined the garrison. They were led by another living legend, Davy Crockett. Both Bowie and Crockett were the sons of Irish immigrants, both had made themselves legends and were possibly the most famous men of their day.

Crockett had served in Congress, but after a losing fight over policy with President Jackson, he went west to find a new life in Texas.

Crockett, Bowie and Travis were all more than six feet tall. Each had red hair. Each had the same kind of blue-gray eyes Sam Houston had. The Mexicans called them "killer eyes." As well they might have done!

The Alamo's defenders, like most of the Anglo population in Texas, originally came from the Southern states. Some were farmers, but most were hunters and trappers. Their lives were never easy, and they were tough. Before Santa Anna's siege actually began, one of them rode to Goliad for help. But all they could muster was thirty-two more men like themselves who fought their way through the Mexican lines into the Alamo. And when they did, it was apparent to everyone inside they would never leave there alive.

What they didn't know, nor ever would, was that the State of Texas had formally declared its independence from Mexico.

Santa Anna's cannon pounded the thick Alamo walls for ten days before a single hole was breached. He knew he was losing time in his plan to bring all of Texas to its knees. His officers disagreed with him, but on the morning of March 6, he gave the order to attack.

His army was well-trained, professional, brave. Some had even had experience in European wars. But none of them had ever fought a fight like this one. Their tactic had long since been proven effective. Infantry with fixed bayonets would approach the fort in columns, climb scaling ladders and easily win the day. Easy for Napoleon, maybe, but not even Napoleon had ever come up against the American long rifle. These men inside the fort had been brought up in the hills of Tennessee, the valleys of Kentucky. They were part of a tradition that made sure every seven-year-old boy had a gun and knew how to use it. If they didn't, they probably didn't live to be eight. They were single- shot guns, but long experience with them made the frontiersmen as fast as they were accurate.

As fast as the Mexican soldiers approached, they were no match at all for these marksmen. It was as though there were thousands inside the Alamo. However, little by little, by sheer weight of numbers, the ladders went up and the troops went over the walls. When they got there, they met an enemy with a single-minded determination to kill as many of them as possible. It must have been terrifying to see these huge men attacking with tomahawks, knives, even their bare hands. Eventually, all the defenders were dead. The Alamo had fallen. But so had the morale of the Mexican Army. They counted 1,600 men dead and when they moved on, left 500 wounded. Inside, they found 182 dead defenders whose bodies they burned and dumped into an unmarked common grave.

The new Texas Republic had gained precious time at the Alamo. Time that saved the Republic, to be sure. But it gained something more. From that day on, the Mexicans lost their stomach for fighting these people, who they now called *diablos tejanos*, Devil Texans.

First-time visitors to San Antonio today find it hard to believe that cannon balls couldn't breach the walls of the Alamo. It looks a lot more like a tiny mission church than an impregnable fort. Actually, it's a church they're looking at. When Mexican troops began pouring over the walls, the defenders retreated into the chapel to make their last stand. It's the chapel that has become the shrine to their bravery.

After the Alamo, Texas tangled with the Mexicans again within a few weeks. In one battle, some 350 Texans were taken prisoner and sent to the fort at Goliad. When Santa Anna heard about that, he was furious. "No prisoners!" he ordered. And so the 350 Texans were taken out and shot.

Their massacre, combined with the drama of the Alamo, united Texans as nothing else could have done. It also brought help from all over the United States. The City of Cincinnati, Ohio, for instance sent two six-pound cannons, which were instrumental in Sam Houston's overwhelming victory over the Mexicans at San Jacinto.

It was there, on April 21, slightly more than six weeks after the Alamo fell, that Houston took Santa Anna prisoner after a surprise attack. It effectively ended the war and established Texas as an independent country, a status she enjoyed until the end of 1845, almost ten years later. Sam Houston, naturally, was the new country's first President.

Meanwhile, in Washington, people like Daniel Webster were fighting to have the United States annex Texas. The Texans themselves had voted overwhelmingly for it, too. There was opposition, particularly over the slavery issue, but as Texas grew in population and in wealth, the opposition began to run out of steam. Finally it became an issue in the Presidential election of 1844 and the Democratic candidate, James Polk, made a campaign issue of what he called the "re-annexation of Texas." The idea easily passed Congress, was approved by the people of the Republic of Texas, and on December 29, 1845, President Polk signed the proclamation welcoming Texas into the United States or, rather, "back" into the United States as he was so fond of putting it.

The Government in Mexico City didn't quite see things that way, and a short time later declared war on the United States. There was fighting in Texas again, but when it all ended, a treaty extended the borders of the United States south to the Rio Grande and west to the Pacific. The year was 1848 and the map of the United States was beginning to look quite a bit like it does today.

Once Texas was on the map, the stage was set for the fun to begin.

Now that it wasn't a foreign country any longer, it was more attractive to more Americans and they began pouring into Texas in record numbers, particularly from the Old South. In the years between Statehood and the Civil War, the population grew to four times its original size.

Basically, the Southern farmers found life in Texas similar in a lot of ways to the lives they had left behind. But there was a difference their fathers could have told them about ... Indians. Texas, by that time, was the only state in all of the United States that still had a wild, untamed frontier where violence was still a way of life.

Austin and others had settled in relatively safe areas where hostile Indians hadn't been much of a problem. When the American Government took charge, it moved most of the Indians from East Texas up into Oklahoma. But once civilization advanced to the plains, the going got tougher.

Hard times in the east lured thousands into Texas and the Government did everything it could think of to attract even more. Every new colony, from Eden to Israel, has been well aware of the need to add more people as a means of survival. In early Texas, where there was virtually no money, the economy demanded expansion and the increase in land values it created. The Government gave every citizen of Texas about 4,000 acres. Every immigrant could have 1,200 acres with no strings attached. In either case, they were free to resell it, and many did. The result was that every family in Texas owned their own land, and that was a powerful lure.

Even though the lure was strong, and immigration from Europe into the United States was growing by leaps and bounds, very few foreign-born people found their way directly into Texas. There was a French colony and another of Scandinavians, but in general, most of the new Texans came from other parts of the United States. With one strange exception. A group of noblemen in Germany got together and promoted a scheme that would encourage the local peasants to leave the country and find new lives in America. It made perfect sense; they would extend their influence to the other side of the world and open new markets at the same time, not to mention getting rid of some peasants. They promised free transportation to the New World, plus a farm with a cabin and enough money to tide a family over until the crops came in. The land they were bargaining with was inside Indian country, but they didn't seem to know that, or at least didn't admit they did. It wasn't good farmland, either, and that came as a surprise both to them and their customers.

To set things right, a German prince, complete with a braided uniform and a retinue of servants, arrived in Texas to negotiate for a more hospitable site. He found a place just north of San Antonio and named it New Braunfels, after himself. By then, though, he was nearly bankrupt. He had met a few swindlers along the way, and it gets expensive trooping secretaries and servants across open country. There were 10,000 German immigrants waiting in Galveston to get settled into their new homes and typhus was taking its toll.

The prince solved the problem by going home, but he left the new settlement in charge of an aide, Otfried von Meusebach, whose first act was to change his name to John O. Meusebach. Then he became a Texas citizen and went to work. He spread the community by buying more land, and though the Germans never really found the land of milk and honey they had been promised, they managed well and prospered. They put down roots, and even today German communities are thriving in Texas, and it isn't at all unusual to hear German spoken in many of them.

Meusebach made an agreement with the Comanches that allowed him to expand deep into Indian territory. He argued that his tribe was neither Texan nor Spanish and so should not be counted among the enemies of the Comanche. They agreed, and the treaty was never broken. Some Germans did fall victim to Indian wrath, but it was mostly due to the fact that all white men look alike when you're a Comanche.

Other settlers didn't have that much luck.

In the same year that Texas declared its independence, a hard-shell Baptist preacher named John Parker took thirty people from Tennessee into the country just east of present-day Waco. He built a fort and settled down to raise corn and contemplate the plight of the rest of civilization, bound surely for Hell in his view. One fine day in May, while most of the men were out setting their crops, a party of Comanche braves wheeled up to the fort and asked for meat and fresh water. One of the men bargained with them, but he had an odd feeling something was wrong. Something was. He told the Indians he had no meat and to be on their way. In response, they cut him down with their spears and rushed the fort. Once inside, they killed and scalped the men, including John Parker, and raped the women. Parker's wife, Granny, was one of them. When the Indians rode off, leaving five dead, Granny pulled out the Indian lance that had her pinned to the ground and began to give chase. They had taken her six-year-old son and nine-year-old daughter as prisoners. The boy was ransomed six years later, but ultimately chose to return to the Indians. His sister, Cynthia Ann Parker, grew up and eventually married an Indian chief. Her son, Quanah Parker, was the last of the Comanche chiefs.

The Parker raid wasn't the first, and it was far from the last. In the years before the Civil War, some 200 people were killed by Indians each year. Many more were tortured and lived to tell about it. And their children, like the Parker youngsters, were carried off and made members of the Indian tribes with all the rights and privileges the Indians gave their own natural children. The white men considered that a fate worse than death, of course. Along the frontier, Indians were considered less than human.

When Mirabeau Buonaparte Lamar replaced Sam Houston as President of the Texas Republic, he told his constituents that "... the white man and the red man cannot dwell in harmony together. Nature forbids it." Nothing short of all-out war to drive them off the land was required, he said. And an all-out war was begun.

What Lamar had in mind was to cut off the problem in one bold stroke rather than hacking away at it. What he got was one of the longest wars in American history. It didn't end until nearly forty years later when Quanah Parker led his people into the Indian territory in Oklahoma. In the meantime, thousands died on both sides. And Hollywood got enough plots for hundreds of Western movies.

When they make movies about Texas, they usually make them out west of the Pecos River. It's Texas the way Texas used to be. And, thanks in part to the movies, it's the way most people who don't live there think all of Texas still is.

A native out there once said, "You can lie on your belly and see for miles. 'Course, there ain't nothin' to see. But if there was, you'd see it!" There are towns there where the only residents are the postmaster, the sheriff, the gas station owner, the barkeeper, the motel proprietor and the owner of the general store. And it's the same person. The whole town is usually a single building that serves as a gathering place for people who come to it from hundreds of miles around for supplies and some good conversation.

These days, on a Saturday night, the lure might also be a little country music provided by the management not so much to attract business, as happens in other places, but just for the joy of it. Everybody gets decked out in their best for occasions like that. The men put on clean dungarees, and the women sometimes even wear evening gowns just to break the pattern. At the very least, they wear "jeans." And when the music starts, everybody dances. Even the folks who don't appear to know how.

But what people are mostly looking for in those crossroads they call towns is good conversation. They live in an area where there's an average of one person for every square mile, so human companionship is important. But even in the big cities of Texas, good conversation is a fine art. From the very beginning Texas had had a high literacy rate, and with it a passion for politics. When Texas became a State, ninety-five percent of the people could read and write. There were more than seventy newspapers, including the San Felipe *Telegraph* that was founded by Gail Borden, who later gave up the newspaper business to sell a new idea he had for condensing milk.

As soon as enough settlers were within shouting distance of each other, they established schools and paid for the teacher out of their own pockets. Their textbooks were usually Bibles. Every family had one, so that cut down expenses. The result was that any Texan could hold his own in any argument by quoting Scripture.

In Austin not long ago, a beer garden where a great many of those arguments have taken place over the years was put on the National Register of Historic Places. In the rest of the country, quaint old inns and fine old houses fill the Register, but in Texas, it's a beer garden. But it's entirely appropriate. This is no ordinary beer garden, not by anybody's standards. Scholz Garten was established in the 1860s and it hasn't closed since, not even during Prohibition. In the early days, it advertised itself as "The oasis of Texas' most exciting intellectuals ... and their women." In 1914 it was bought by a German singing society, and singing is still very important there. If a group of customers decides to burst into song, as they often do, you're given a choice by the management of joining them or leaving quietly.

It's a favorite hangout for politicians from the Statehouse down the street as well as partisans of the Texas A&M football team and the University of Texas football team. With a mix like that, you're bound to get a lot of friendly discussions, and that's what makes Scholz's fun. According to some regulars, the greatest debate the place has ever seen happened ten years ago between Fletcher Boone and Martin Wigginton over the nature of man. Man is just interested in bread alone, said Wigginton. But he needs beauty, too, argued Boone. Five hours and fifteen rounds of beer later, neither had convinced the other. There was no agreement among the crowd of spectators, either. But if they felt any thirst, it was only for truth.

Out in West Texas, the sounds of discussions like that are sometimes the only sounds to be heard. It's a quiet country with few animal sounds, very little traffic, and hardly ever even the gentle sound of rain. It rained there back in 1950. But not again for seven years. The price of cattle dropped from $250 a head to $65 and a lot of ranchers sold out. But most hung on and still do, even though they know they'll never get rich. For one thing, they find great beauty in this land with its harsh sun and strong wind and breathtaking vistas. For another, they don't like cities. Or city folks. They like not having to own an umbrella. They don't mind it when the temperature goes over a hundred degrees. But they don't much care for those "Easterners" who come in from Houston and try to buy their ranches for tax shelters.

Out there they don't have enough income to have much truck with taxes. The average income for the whole state is under $8,500 a year. In most places west of the Pecos, it's about half that. Everybody knows everybody else and everybody cares. So nobody goes hungry. They don't, that is unless nothing will do but a McDonald's hamburger or a Kentucky Fried Chicken breast. Though there are thousands of miles of highways west of the Pecos, there are virtually no fast food outlets along them. Oh, occasionally you'll see an electric sign that says EATS, but the food inside is probably tacos and chili and probably home-cooked. There are bright lights, too, usually out over the local high school football field, and that, on a night a game is scheduled, is where you'll find everybody from miles around.

Football is a disease among Texans. People who don't play it at least talk about it, and it's a rare Texan who doesn't have something to say about the sport. Every town takes pride in its high school team, and everyone has a favorite college team. And to fill in the time when neither high school nor college has a team on the field, they've got two teams in the National Football League.

Almost as famous as the Dallas Cowboys are the Dallas Cowboys Cheerleaders, which is part of another Texas tradition. Every major town in Texas has a contingent of cheerleaders to go with its football team and they compete with each other as much as the teams themselves. It's enough to make outsiders believe what every Texan is sure to tell you during the first hour of your friendship: Texas women are the most beautiful and charming to be found anywhere in the world. Anybody who argues with that is surely a fool, and almost certainly not a Texan.

More than in almost any other region of the world, women stand large in local Texas legend. Down on the Rio Grande in West Texas, the little town of Langtry keeps alive one of the most fascinating of all those stories.

In the center of town there's a tourist attraction called "The Judge Roy Bean Law West of The Pecos Museum." It's a combination bar and courtroom where the judge held court back around the turn of the century. When Roy Bean arrived there and built a general store, the town was a camp for the construction gangs who were building the Southern Pacific Railroad. They were a rowdy bunch, and officials of the railroad thought they needed a justice of the peace. As a businessman, Bean was the "establishment," and the popular choice for the job. In good weather, his court was in session on the front porch of the local saloon, which was built, as often happens in Texas to this day, as an extension of his general store. He liked handing out justice on the front porch. It was cool there and he never lacked an audience. If it was rainy or cold, so much the better. A good trial was good for the saloon business, so he moved the court inside. If the perpetrator insisted on a jury trial, why, almost anybody at the bar would serve gladly.

They called Roy Bean the "hanging judge," but to set the record straight here and now, he was a gentle man who never hanged anyone. It was true he hated horse thieves. Everybody did. But he didn't ever hang them. Instead, he took everything they had, including the horses they had allegedly stolen and sent them on their way. Their money went into the day's saloon receipts.

The name of Bean's saloon was "The Jersey Lilly," and it was a tribute to the romantic side of his nature. The poor man was hopelessly in love with a beautiful actress named Lily Langtry. He named the town for her and started a letter-writing blitz to lure her to visit him. Possibly because he spelled her name wrong, or possibly because there was a long line ahead of him, the great Jersey Lily didn't get around to answering any of his letters. But she did go to Langtry in 1904. Not long after Judge Roy Bean had cashed in his chips.

If Bean and his counterparts thought they were the only law west of the Pecos, they weren't fooling anybody but themselves. Everybody knew then, as they do now, about the Texas Rangers.

You don't have to go back to the thrilling days of yesteryear to meet up with the Rangers – they're alive and well in all parts of Texas. Men join the Texas Highway Patrol with nothing more in mind than to graduate from there into the Rangers, but most of them just wind up spending the rest of their days cruising the endless highways that run in straight lines all over the State. Once in a while one of them makes it, but the entire Ranger force these days is less than a hundred men, and it's not a job a man gives up, even though the pay isn't too spectacular. The pay never was very good, but the payoff in pride is legendary.

A few years ago, the Chief of the Rangers described his force as: "dedicated, humble, kindly men of honesty and integrity. They are fearless, courageous and tough when the occasion demands." And they live by one simple rule, he added: "You'd better not ever do anything to bring discredit to the Rangers."

What the Texas Rangers have that few other law-enforcement agencies can imitate is tradition. Organized only seven years after Bobbies started patrolling the streets of London and nearly forty years before the Royal Canadian Mounted Police began calming things down in the Northwest Territories, the history of the Texas Rangers is part and parcel with the history of Texas itself.

In the beginning, the settlers couldn't afford to pay a regular army, nor could they afford the time away from their farms to protect themselves, so they organized a company of men who were part police, part soldier. They didn't have a regular base, but "ranged" to wherever they were needed. They were kept very busy indeed. There wasn't much in the way of Government money to pay them, and so their care and feeding, as well as their recruitment, was up to the frontiersmen themselves. In some ways, they were like the roving knights of another era. Since they were all volunteers, they were all more courageous and adventuresome than the average. And if a man were to rise among them to become a Ranger Captain, chances are he was an absolutely fearless man. The enemy, to them, were Mexican and Indian, and had them hopelessly outnumbered. The result was that a Texas Ranger was a very cautious man. They fought with guerrilla tactics, and with numbers against them, it was better to take the offensive. And that made the Rangers aggressive as well as cautious, a fascinating combination.

They understood their enemy very well and knew how to seize the advantage. They used psychology in another way, too. They used their own legend of invulnerability as a very good defense. After a few years of fighting, everyone – the people they defended and the ones they fought – treated them with a healthy respect. And they seem to have deserved it.

But as good as they were, the war would probably still be going on today except for something that happened in Paterson, New Jersey, of all places. One Samuel Colt, who had only recently toured the country taking culture to the people with demonstrations of laughing gas, established a new company he called the "Patent Arms Manufacturing Company." It would make and, hopefully, sell his new invention, a revolving pistol that could fire six shots without stopping to reload.

Colt's years as a self-styled "doctor" on the scientific lecture circuit had taught him the principles of promotion. He made presentation models of his gun for such people as President Jackson. But, except for a few sales to Army officers as novelties, the world didn't seem ready for a six-shooter in 1839.

The Texas Rangers were, though.

Rangers usually carried a rifle and a shotgun and a single-shot pistol. When they got involved in a fight, they had to get off their horses and fight on foot. The Indians, meanwhile, fought very well from the backs of their horses. The Rangers needed the same advantage.

Colt had sold some repeating rifles to the Texas Navy and in the process had interested some of the Rangers in his revolving pistols. One of his apostles, Ranger Rip Ford, said of it, "The six-shooter, when properly handled, is the only weapon. Mind you, sir, I say when properly handled."

The first to handle it properly was Ranger Captain Jack Hays. He was a twenty-three-year-old man from Tennessee who had drifted into Texas to become a surveyor, but became a Ranger instead. He also became a legend. For the next hundred years every Texas Ranger wanted nothing more than "to be like Jack Hays."

One day when he was patrolling the Pedernales River with a force of fourteen Rangers, he was jumped by a Comanche war party. Hays' troop fought on horseback and killed thirty of the seventy Indians. Significantly, it was the first time they were able to fight from their horses. The six-shooter had made it possible.

Within weeks Hays and his men were attacked again by a force much larger than themselves. This time they were surprised while camped in the Neuces canyon. Hays answered their volleys of arrows with rifle fire. But then he surprised the Indians by ordering his men to mount up and charge. The Comanches had never seen anything like it before. Usually the white men either looked for cover or turned and ran. These men were charging!

The Indians weren't the sort to run from a fight so they made a stand. But these crazy white men were breaking all the standard rules. They kept coming, shouting and yelling and, strangest of all, spitting fire from their hands. And Indians were falling from their horses. Confused, they turned and ran. And the Rangers ran after them. The chase went on for three miles before the Indians threw down their weapons and gave up the fight. Their leader said: "I will never again fight Jack Hays, who has a shot for every finger on the hand."

It wasn't long before the Indians adopted new tactics and the war went on in spite of the six-shooter. But Hays gave them a lot to think about. His tactic was to find Indian camps by watching for buzzards who always circled over them no matter how well-hidden they were. Then he'd attack while they were still asleep. Even without his revolver, Hays would have become a legend. As one Indian chief put it: "Me and Red Wing not afraid to go to hell together. Captain Jack heap brave. Not afraid to go to hell by himself!"

He was tough on Mexicans, too. They offered a reward of $500 in silver for his head. The Texans loved it, pointing out that this twenty-five-year-old man only weighed 160 pounds. The reward was heavier than he was.

The pistol Hays used was more of a novelty than a perfect weapon. Though it shot six bullets without reloading, it had to be taken apart to reload, which was pretty hard to do while you were riding a horse. The gun was too light and not perfectly balanced. And worse, the bore was only .34 calibre, making it more frightening than deadly.

Another Texas Ranger, Captain Samuel Walker, went up to New York and worked with Colt on modifying the gun to make it more useful. He made it bigger and stronger. He increased the bore to .44 calibre, and he made the grip easier to hold in a big Texan hand. He added a thick trigger guard so it could be slipped into a belt, and, most important, added a rammer under the barrel so it could be reloaded without taking it apart.

Because it was heavier, Walker said, it made a dandy club to use on people who "aren't worth shooting."

The new gun, called the Walker Colt, was the gun that won the West. It probably killed more men than any handgun ever made.

And, as is probably typical of "civilized" societies, the gun made heroes of the men who killed with them. Everyone in the East knew about the Rangers and their guns. They admired their camaraderie and the fact they preferred not to talk but to act. They viewed them as decent men, not given to boasting, who never looked for trouble, but never ran from it, either. Their courage was legendary, their skill taken for granted. And if they killed a lot of people, what of it? They were killing Mexicans and Indians, and most Americans didn't think of either as "people."

They were the first of the great Western heroes. And today, thanks to the legends that were built then, we think of them as "cowboys," and the image is interchangeable. They made cowboys possible, to be sure. But compared to the Rangers, cowboys are Johnny-come-latelies on the Texas scene.

There were huge cattle ranches in Mexico and a few in Texas before the Civil War, but what would become cattle country was at that time rich in buffalo. And in the hands of the Comanche. The prairie was huge and intimidating and the Indians were determined to keep it as their own. The Texas Rangers and the U.S. Cavalry had their hands full. But the Indians weren't too interested in the territory below San Antonio, and it was in that triangle bounded by San Antonio, the Rio Grande and the Gulf that the early cattle kingdoms were formed.

The Mexicans to the south, on the other hand, felt in constant danger from Indians, and many of the big rancheros had fled for their lives, leaving their longhorns behind to fend for themselves. It was easy for them. So easy in fact, they reproduced in record numbers and the American farmers who settled in Southern Texas found them a nuisance.

But some of the new Texans didn't see it that way at all. Richard King and Mifflin Kenedy, for instance, both came down from the North seeking fortunes as traders on the Rio Grande. In the process, they got control of huge tracts of land and millions of head of wild cattle everyone else considered pests.

There wasn't much market for them, nor any easy way to ship cattle, so the "industry" grew rather slowly. In the beginning, for people like the Kings and Kenedys, the acquisition of land was the important thing, and they did that with a vengeance.

But when the Civil War ended, everything changed. Railroads began to move west, cities in the North began to mushroom, more people could afford meat and began to demand it. The longhorn steers were just what the market ordered. They were tough enough to walk a thousand miles or more across the desert to the railroads up north in Kansas and Missouri.

The drama of the cattle drives fired everyone's imagination, and it brought money into Texas, something there was too little of in those days. The farmers whose lands they crossed weren't too pleased to see them. The land itself was hostile, and there were thieves along the way. Yet for all the danger and potential for excitement, the average cattle drive was probably no more exciting than driving a truck across the country.

Some 200 herds a year made the trek. Each herd had about 2,500 head of cattle in the care of about a dozen cowboys. They took along five or six horses for each man and the whole company was followed by a supply wagon, remembered by fans of Western novels as a "chuck" wagon. Assuming there were no special problems a herd could move as much as fifteen miles a day. The average cost per steer for the whole trip was about fifty cents, much cheaper than it would have been to ship the cattle any other way than under their own steam.

Usually, they camped out at night along the way, and most often the campsites were also the site of a well. Today those wells are still the center of activity for people who live out on the prairie. They've been replaced by roadside stores that sell gas for the pickup trucks everyone seems to own. But they're something much more than gas stations. They're general stores, saloons, meat markets, motels and dance halls all housed under a single roof. On Friday nights people gather there from miles around to restock their larders and to recharge their mental batteries with a little gossip, a little story-telling, a lot of companionship.

The best known of all the trails out of Texas was the Chisholm Trail beginning at the Red River and running across Indian country into Kansas. It was blazed by Jesse Chisholm, a Cherokee, who supplied beef to the Army posts in the Indian Territory. At the other end was Abilene, Kansas, a place Texans put on the map.

When the cowboys got there and the cattle were sold they collected their pay, about thirty dollars for each month's work. It was a fortune! And there were plenty of ways to spend it in Abilene. There were saloons for instance; lots of them. And a man does get thirsty on the trail. If they were looking for a fight, that was easy. Most of the Texas cowboys had roots in the deep South and still had scars from the Civil War. To keep order, the Abilene city fathers hired marshals from the North who also had scars from the Civil War. Oh yes, finding a fight was easy!

If wind and rain, dust and ornery critters made a cowboy's life hard, there were other irritations too, not the least of them Indians. Before the longhorn, there were buffalo, and though the major cattle trails skirted farm country generally, they ran straight across the Indian hunting grounds. But other white men were at work on that "problem."

Back East, buffalo robes had become all the rage. They were fashionable enough to bring high prices, and Texas had another cash crop. The trading post at Fort Worth was the center of the activity, and tough mountain men fanned out from there onto the plains. They worked together in groups of ten or more with heavy rifles and wagon-loads of ammunition. A good man could kill as many as fifty buffalo a day, and their rifles allowed them to do it from a safe distance. Once they had killed off a herd, they moved onto the next one. Hide wagons followed them and skinners stripped off the hides, leaving the carcasses to rot in the sun.

It was a bloody business and the men who played the game were tough characters. They attracted others like them who played different games. Poker players, dance hall girls, prostitutes and con men poured in to get their share of the profits. Their camps were boom towns where anything could be had for the right price.

Tales of the adventure on the plains lured more white men there, and it became a great sport to fire into the buffalo herds from passing trains. It didn't take long to decimate the herds. Or for the Indians to react.

The Army had traditionally taken a defensive role against Indians in Texas. But when the buffalo slaughter made the Indians more savage, the policy changed and Lamar's war took on a new meaning. Both sides had a new determination, but for the Indians, the end was in sight.

The Comanches attacked a hunter's fort called Adobe Walls in the spring of 1874. They were badly mauled in the fight, but moved on across the plains killing any hunters who crossed their path. The hunting season ended and the last chapter in the Indian War began. The Army went on the march with orders to break up any Indian camps they found. Finding camps wasn't that easy. More often the Indians found soldiers. But after all those years, the white man had learned a little something about the red man. And the most important thing was that Indians always took their women and children with them when they fought a war. They couldn't be beaten in open country. But if their main camp could be found, that would be a different story.

The American leader, Colonel Ranald Mackenzie, understood his enemy very well. He fought like an Indian himself; doggedly, patiently, quietly. But, though he knew it existed, he couldn't find the Comanche camp.

Then one day he took a prisoner. The man was a Comanchero, part Mexican, part Indian, a breed despised by white men and red alike. The prisoner was persuaded to talk and told them where to find the hidden camp.

It was in the Panhandle, a sea of high grass that went on forever. When Mackenzie's scouts arrived there, they were convinced the prisoner had lied. But the plain was laced with deep canyons, and it was inside one of them they spotted it. Far below, spread out along a stream for three miles or more was a huge camp with hundreds of horses and Indian teepees. They reported back to Mackenzie who then marched 600 soldiers overnight to reach the camp at dawn.

The scouts attacked first, killing the sentries, and the cavalry followed. But before they could form a line, the Indians had been warned. Mackenzie was ready for that; his first order was to stampede their horses. Without their mounts, the Comanche braves were at a serious disadvantage. The Indians delayed the soldiers with heavy fire, allowing their women and children to escape, then, before the white men could follow, they turned and ran themselves.

Mackenzie hadn't intended to run after them. Instead he burned their camp to the ground. Then he ordered their horses rounded up and shot. Although only four Indians had been killed in the raid, they were thoroughly beaten. Without horses they couldn't fight. Worse, they couldn't find food. Some went north to the reservations in Oklahoma and those who stayed were worn down by Mackenzie in an unprecedented winter war.

In the spring, their chief, Quanah Parker, took the last of his people to the government reservations. He continued to lead his people until he died in 1911.

Without buffalo to eat the grass or Indians to harass the cowboys, the cattle kingdoms expanded by leaps and bounds. Where the Indians had staged their great buffalo hunts, the spectacle had become the annual cattle roundup. All the land, technically, belonged to the state, and the custom was for a man to go into open country and run his cattle. The steers of different owners ran together and it was necessary to separate them once a year before the drive to market. Cattle were branded, and calves were given the same brand as their mothers, so it was fairly simple to tell who owned what.

The ranch owners were as tough and hardworking as the men who worked for them. They could ride and shoot and curse with the best of them. It wasn't a life well-suited to just anyone. You had to be tough and resilient and you had to have a healthy respect for the land. They were mostly very young and their youthful exuberance is very much a part of the Texas character today.

You can generally spot a Texan in the big cities of the North because they usually wear big hats. A Texan explains: "Down here in this country, you'd just as soon do without boots as not wear a hat. Why, a hat is a bare necessity!" Cowboys wear them to protect the neck and head from the hot sun and the face from the rain and sleet. They're terrific buckets, if you're lucky enough to find a water hole. For a snooze after lunch, tilt the brim over your face and presto! It's night-time. A big hat is good for keeping bugs off your face. And there's nothing like it to wave in the air to get lazy longhorns moving.

Contrary to popular belief, not all Western hats look alike. And in Texas, they mark a man by the hat he wears. Ask a cattle trader: "If you walk into a trading session with the wrong kind of hat," he'll tell you, "it makes you look like some kind of fool. Well, you're just going to get taken, that's all."

Generally, cowhands buy a new hat every year and pay up to $125 for the image. Once they've poked it and crushed it into the shape they think suits them best, they spray it with sugar water and starch to keep it that way. Then they set out to get it dirty. When they put it on or take it off, they always use the same fingers in the same spot to get finger marks on the brim. This, they say, marks them as a true cowhand because dudes never think of that.

You can spot a dude by the angle of his Western hat, too. Real cowboys never wear them at a jaunty angle because they know the wind would whip them away if they did. On the other hand, if a real cowboy has been drinking, you can tell how much he's had by the angle of his hat.

Today's cowboy might not be a cowboy at all, but a great many people in Texas do everything they can to keep the image alive. Some say they're more Texan than Old Texas itself. In the big cities like Houston, they call them "kickers." You see dozens every day racing along the freeways in their pickup trucks wearing cowboy hats, with a chaw in their cheeks, a long-neck bottle of Lone Star beer in their hands and a Willie Nelson tape, turned up very loud, on the eight-track. No matter that they may work as computer programmers at the Houston Space Center, they've got the spirit of the Old West about them!

It seems everybody wears cowboy hats and Lone Star belt buckles, boots with pointed toes and high heels and drink their beer straight from the bottle. They adore country music and they dance steps Billy the Kid would have felt comfortable with. Yes, the spirit of the West lives on in the cities of Texas.

But a huge percentage of the people who live in the cities of Texas are Yankees. There are fortunes to be made in the Southwest these days, and Texas is at the center of the action. They arrive in large numbers and many quickly adapt to the traditions of their new home. The Texas character is exuberant and spicy, friendly and buoyant, gallant and well-mannered. It's an easy style to adopt, and those who do are the lucky ones. A native Houstonian explained how it happens: "At first they think it's corny. Then they begin to wear boots and blue jeans. Then they find it's great fun to go out and drink honky-tonk beer. After a while, they go to visit Mama and Daddy up east, and they see that people there don't understand Texans. That one trip can change "them" to "us."

But what would Sam Houston think of the city that bears his name? It's surely a city with a future and it's about as close to anything America has that could be called an "instant city." Most of the world's cities are built at the edge of a mountain, along a river or at the head of a harbor. Houston was built at the junction of two bayous by a couple of New York real estate speculators. It's fifty miles from the coast, but that was no problem, they built a canal to make it a seaport. Then they built highways. Miles and miles of highways. The center city's 200-square-mile area is ringed by a freeway they call Loop 610. If you go less than seventy miles an hour on it, someone is sure to blow his horn and call you a "farmer." If you live in Houston, you need a car, and when you drive you're on a freeway more than half the time.

There are no zoning laws in Houston. Growth is all that counts. The result is that every architectural style popular in the last fifty years spreads out in every direction. It's hard to find its center. "Downtown" on Main Street, huge office towers with names like Shell Plaza, Pennzoil Place, Tenneco and Humble give the city a feeling of power and substance. In spite of all the space around them, they're usually connected by underground tunnels. It gets hot in Houston, and people prefer to stay indoors as much as they can. Out along the freeways, huge enclosed shopping centers have sprouted up along the interchanges. People drive right into the center garages and can live their whole lives without ever going outdoors.

One of the most spectacular of them, the Post Oak Galleria, is a huge three-level shopping center that includes offices, hotels and a giant skating rink with a glass roof. It's the place to see and be seen in Houston. For sports, the place to see is the Astrodome, another indoor spectacle with its own artificial environment. They call it the "Astrodomain," and it includes everything from a stone chapel to a shooting gallery.

Along the freeways, you'll find just about anything you're looking for and you don't have to look too hard because the used car lots, the restaurants, the finance companies have all conspired to put up signs to attract your attention as you zip by at sixty miles an hour. The used car lots and gas stations seem to prefer pennants, adding both color and motion to the scene. A restaurant displays a giant lobster with a pair of six-guns, cowboy hats in every size and shape are etched in neon, plaster statues revolve in the splendor of pastel spotlights. By comparison, Los Angeles is a dowdy old woman.

But for all that, there's a symmetry about Houston that makes it work. It's open and free, populated by people eager to make it. It's one of the few cities in the world where a man can watch the moon rise over a park and say, with perfect honesty, that he has explored both. Houston is the home of America's space program, and that, more than anything else, makes it a very real symbol of America's present. And its future. And don't let anybody tell you it isn't exciting!

While people in the cities may have traded their horses for a motorcycle and a bass fishing boat and live in Tudor houses in the suburbs or in glass towers or singles apartment complexes, their grandfathers probably lived in log cabins. Not much more than a hundred years ago, most Texans lived in homes they called "dog- runs." It was actually two separate log cabins connected by a continuous roof. The space between was for the dogs. Sanitary facilities for the people were usually the nearest woods. The house often had a front porch, which doubled as extra storage space and a place for men and dogs to get in out of the sun. They were built of logs held together by mud. The chimneys were made of sticks, also held together by mud, and every family kept a long pole handy to topple the chimney when it caught fire, as it inevitably did.

Nobody lives in dog-run cabins any more and homes without indoor plumbing are rare. But the style of life the early settlers knew hasn't changed much in the Piney Woods of East Texas. For a lot of families house trailers have replaced the old log cabins, and many of those who live in small cabins or shanties have added TV antennae to the roof. But they still live cut off from the world, and from their neighbors, deep in the thick woods. They still hunt for squirrels by day and 'coons by night, and they fish for bass and catfish with canepoles. Each family owns a pack of dogs, possibly a mule or two and a cow, some chickens, hogs and a goat. They earn their living cutting trees, but they mostly live off the land.

The original pioneers brought their eating habits from other parts of the South. They didn't plant gardens or fruit trees and thought of milk as a thing only babies drank. They weren't even sure it was really good for them. Almost without exception, from family to family and from day to day, they ate fried salt pork, hot corn bread, sweet potatoes and molasses. And almost without exception, their children suffered from pellagra.

In the Piney Woods today, the standard diet is a little more varied, a little bit healthier. But not much more of either. A lot of their food grows wild in the woods and swamps, and they're more willing to grow their own than their grandfathers were. They have eggs, too, and lots of squirrels, which they eat fried. They raise collard greens and peas, watermelon, potatoes, cabbages and sugar cane. They grow corn, of course, but mainly feed it to the hogs and the mules. And, like their ancestors, they have what almost amounts to a lust for hot corn bread and syrup.

If you are what you eat, food may be another valuable clue to the Texas state of mind. Someone once said that the fry-pan probably killed more Texas pioneers than the Comanche. But if there's a message there, it hasn't registered with anyone in Texas. If you order a steak in a restaurant, you'll get it fried. If you order almost anything else from venison to fish, you'll probably get it barbecued. Now, a lot of people consider a Texas barbecue a wonder to behold. And it is, in the right company and as long as there's plenty to drink. But basically, the idea was originally conceived as a way to make stringy grass-fed beef palatable. Usually, the meat is boiled for a long time to make it tender. Since that also takes away the flavor, it's necessary to put flavor back. The process starts with vinegar, oil, salt and pepper, but then imagination takes over and just about everybody in Texas has his own "secret" recipe.

But there's another kind of food Texas is famous for, and the fame is well deserved. Back before the turn of the century, when the open-air market in the Plaza in San Antonio shut down each night, women set up boards on sawhorses, covered them with oilcloth and sold chili con carne, enchiladas, tamales and other tasty treats we now call "Tex-Mex" food. There "chili queens" sold a bowl of chili for a dime, and gave you bread and water free in the bargain. Their influence spread nationwide with a San Antonio Chili Stand at the Century of Progress World's Fair in Chicago in 1839. It spread faster a few years later when a Texas businessman concocted and canned commercial chili powder. The enthusiasm hasn't stopped, in spite of the fact that the Mayor of San Antonio ran the Chili Queens out of town in 1939, calling them a public health menace.

Of course, people with tender digestive systems might agree that Tex-Mex is a public health menace. But that's their problem. They miss the sheer joy of well-prepared chili con carne, the tang of a tamale, the satisfaction of a plate of refried beans, the fun of a taco, the pleasure of an enchilada. It's one of the gifts Texas has given America, but it's still at its best only in Texas.

All the big cities in Texas have their landmark Mexican restaurants. But often better are the places that began in Mexican homes in the smaller towns. It was once customary for Mexican women who were known for their talent in the kitchen to have an open house one day a week, serving their specialties to the neighbors. It became a small business for many of them, and their establishments were called "Fonditas," or small inns.

But if food is important to Texas, so is drink. If Texas were still an independent country, it would rank in the top fifteen of the world in beer consumption. The food seems to demand it, of course, but huge quantities of beer are consumed over endless games of dominoes as well as in some of the most glamorous pool halls in the world. Beer is what lubricates long evenings of conversation and arguing. And when you sing a lot, as Texans do at the drop of a ten-gallon hat, nothing wets your whistle like a frosty cold beer.

Ironically, however, you can't get a cold beer everywhere in Texas. Imagine where it would stand in the statistics if you could! There are a lot of "church people" in Texas, fundamentalist Christians who take a dim view of such frivolity as dancing and card playing, going to the movies – even Western movies – on Sunday, and, most of all, drinking. Many cities and counties forbid it by law, In fact, there's probably more prohibition in Texas than in any other state today.

Texas leads the country in a lot of other categories, too. Some eighty percent of all American beef comes from Texas ranches. About the same percentage of wool and mohair comes from Texas sheep herds. More computer software comes from Texas, and only one other state provides more electronic parts.

And, of course there's all that oil.

Oil put Texas on the map. It also spawned a lot of tall tales like the one about the cattle rancher who had the misfortune to find oil on his spread in North Texas. "Damn it," he said, "cattle can't drink that stuff!" It also made quite a few millionaires, and more tall tales about Texas.

The simple fact is, more people in Texas don't have oil wells than do. But that's not to say most people don't benefit from them no matter where they live or what they do. The State collects so many millions from its oil and natural gas industry, there's no need for a personal income tax, as there is in most states. And real estate taxes are among the lowest in the country. And there's always hope. Not long ago, a maker of oil well parts decided to advertise his line on television. At the end, the sexy young saleswoman, as if admitting not everyone in her audience is a prospect, purrs into the camera: "If y'all don't have an awl well ... git one!"

The "awl bidniss," as it's known in Texas, began at Beaumont in 1901 in a field called Spindletop. It blew oil all over the place. And before long more fields were discovered, but nobody was jumping for joy. The oil business in those days was supplying fuel for lamps, and Texas crude had lighter hydrocarbons that were more volatile, and when it was used in lamps it blew them up.

But that didn't stop the promoters. Even though the price of oil dropped to about three cents a barrel, the cost of land in Beaumont went over $100,000 an acre. And though wags everywhere were calling it "Swindletop," the promoters didn't have any problem finding investors.

Then along came Henry Ford. The automobile, with its internal combustion engine, was just what Texas ordered. If Texas crude blew up lamps, that made it perfect for making gasoline and the search was on for more. In just a few years, oil was discovered under just about every county in Texas, and the Lone Star State was the country's top oil producer in 1928. After having been so poor for so long, it was a wonderful thing.

But that was just the beginning. In 1930, a wildcatter named "Dad" Joiner, who had been searching for oil in East Texas for years, brought in a well that made it all worthwhile. He had discovered a field about six miles wide and forty-two miles long. It has produced well over three billion barrels by now and it's not dry yet.

Joiner had made strikes before, but he was seventy years old and dead broke when he hit the big one. He had sunk two dry holes and had to borrow a rig to try a third, financing it with pieces of the well. He went down to 3,400 feet and was about to give up when she blew. A fountain of oil flooded the field around him and "Dad" Joiner knew he was a rich man.

He moved to Dallas and the first thing he did was divorce his wife and marry a much younger woman. His children, among many others, sued him for all he was worth. And when he died ten years later, at eighty, he was broke again. But happy. You can be sure of that.

The farmers and ranchers who owned the land made fortunes in royalties, and they began to whisper among themselves that an oil well or two made ranching a fine business. It made a lot of men rich in a hurry. Some eighty percent of the major strikes were made by wildcatters like Joiner, and once they made a fortune, they didn't mind risking it on new ventures. More conservative Northern businessmen never could understand that part of the Texas character. But the "easy come, easy go" attitude of the Texans was based on simple fact. The Texan knew if he lost his fortune he could make another. After all, he was broke when he started, wasn't he? And his associates usually agreed with the philosophy, so they stuck together in bad times as well as good. That made for more good times than bad. And a lot of bankers up North are still scratching their heads over that idea.

The oil boom attracted a breed that could pass for a reincarnation of the pioneers, the cowboys or the buffalo hunters. They called them roughnecks because almost no other name fits so well. Generally they were big, strong, tough. They handled two-foot steel pipe as though it were made of aluminum and, like the cowboys themselves, didn't seem to mind wind or rain, hot sun or snow. They drank hard whiskey with the same enthusiasm and they chased wild women. And if you were looking for a fight, they'd give you one gladly. If you needed some expensive drilling equipment, you could order it from some of them. And many nights, if you wanted to find one of them, the local jail would probably be a good place to look.

Many have been replaced by machines. And though you have to be tough to survive in the oil fields today, the high adventure that attracted the early roughnecks has gone out of the business.

The old entrepreneurs have largely been replaced by corporate types, too. Nothing stays the same. Not even Texas.

But some things, thankfully, do stay the same. One of them is Big Bend National Park and the territory that surrounds it along the Rio Grande in West Texas. The park is bounded on one side by the huge Big Bend Ranch and on the other by canyons, where the river gets every bit as wild as the Colorado as it rushes through the Grand Canyon.

They are still in the same state they were when the first white man went west, and together they give a good idea of the variety of experience the pioneers encountered.

The canyons, a short distance downstream from the park, take about a week to explore, and the only way it can be done is in a small canoe. And once you begin the trip, there's nothing else you can do but finish it. There's no way out but downstream. The early explorers chose to go around the canyons, and not many Indians went in, either. Even today, the trip is considered too dangerous for most people, and so it's an experience few people have had. The result is that nothing in the canyons has changed in recorded history. The brave souls who do take the trip find themselves cut off from the world by cliffs a thousand feet over their heads and propelled along by rushing white water. Herons, eagles and falcons fly overhead, mountain lions hunt among the rocks. And, except for the sound the water makes, it's an utterly peaceful, quiet journey back in time.

Another spectacular canyon, Colorado Canyon in the Big Bend Ranch area, is much more negotiable, but not much less dramatic. Almost every type of water bird has been seen in Colorado Canyon at one time or another. And a lot of modern explorers have seen bears. Almost everyone who canoes through the canyon sees muskrat and beaver. You're likely to see other human beings, too, because the canyon is easy to reach and fairly simple to negotiate.

Not far away is a wonderful waterfall that was virtually unknown to anyone until some surveyors stumbled on it in 1970. It's a pair of cascades tumbling some 150 feet into a lush garden of cottonwoods and willows that keep the pool below shaded and cool. All around it the land is hostile and dry, almost desert, but the Madrid Falls offer an island of life. Water from them runs down through a lush valley surrounded on both sides by high, and very dry, canyon walls.

The Indians knew it was there, of course; the Spaniards passed it by. The Americans used it as an oasis on the trail, but nobody seriously considered living there. So there it stands today, as beautiful as it was the day the first man arrived, and as untouched.

Spend time with any Texan and you're sure to come away with the impression they're a people deeply rooted to the land. In many ways, they are. But except for a few spots where nature itself stepped in and made it impossible, or, at the very least, the Government had made it illegal, it's always been the Texans' nature to change the land. The fact that this may have been the toughest land in the world to tame is a tribute to them. But the real story of Texas is more to be found in the people than in the land.

The Texas story is Sam Houston and Steven Austin dedicating their lives to building a new way of life. It's the story of Davy Crockett, who became as much a Texan as any man who ever lived, even though he only lived there a week or so. It's men like Richard King, who arrived in Texas with hopes of becoming a merchant prince and wound up building the biggest cattle ranch in the world.

People who don't know much about Texas usually know one thing for sure; that it was originally settled by people running away from debtors, by gamblers and thieves, murderers and other assorted riffraff ... which shows how much *they* know.

The truth is, the early Texans were no more lawless or uncouth than any other pioneers. There were a lot of saloons in Texas, and it was never hard to find a friendly game of chance. But in those days, such things were considered more forms of entertainment than vice, not only in Texas, but in most parts of the United States.

They were very religious people, generally. Each family owned land and was forced to work hard on it. There wasn't time to get into trouble, and there were few reasons for lawlessness. In fact, in 1844 a local newspaper reported: "The County Jail has for some time been without tenants. There is not a single bullying, disorderly citizen, not even a loafer to be seen in the city or county. It is also the case in the counties adjoining."

Of course, there were some bad apples. Sam Bass was one of them, but everybody loved him for it. Sam was a train robber. In one holdup, he took more gold than he or his men could carry. Sam was a Yankee, which was bad news in Texas after the Civil War. But he charmed the natives so well, it showed Texans for the first time that Yankees aren't all bad. Robbing trains was exciting for Sam, and he found stagecoaches great fun. But they were all moving targets and not nearly as easy to knock over as banks. Sam switched to banks. And that was his downfall.

One hot day in July, 1878, Sam and three of his cronies rode into Round Rock to make a withdrawal from the local bank. And they ran right into a Texas Ranger. The Ranger thought he noticed the outline of a gun under Sam's coat. He walked up to him and touched the bulge. Politely (Rangers are always polite!), he asked Sam if that might be a gun in there.

"You bet it is," said Sam. And used it on the Ranger right then and there.

The noise attracted a second Ranger, who drew his gun and fired. The bullets took two fingers off Sam's hand, but he gave as good as he took, and the Ranger had a bullet in his lung. That didn't stop the Ranger, though. He kept on coming. And he was followed by four more Rangers and a few helpful citizens.

Sam and his boys ran down an alley, but before they could reach their horses, Sam took another bullet in the stomach. One of his partners took one in the head. Another of his pals, who wasn't hurt, climbed into his saddle and pulled Sam up after him. Then, firing all the while, they rode off out of town. They went three miles or more before Sam had to call it quits. His friend wanted to stay and help him shoot it out with the Rangers, who were already in sight.

But Sam refused the offer. "I'm done for," he said.

When the Rangers caught up, all the fight was out of poor Sam. They took him back into town, bound up his wounds, and started asking all kinds of questions, mainly about where his pals might be.

But Sam Bass didn't talk. "If a man knows anything," he said, "he ought to die with it." And with that, Sam died. With his boots on, as they say down in Texas.

There were a lot of cattle thieves in Texas in the old days, too. But in defense of the Texans, they were more often the victims. Most of the rustlers were Mexicans. Longhorns were worth as much as eighteen dollars a head in Cuba, and that made it worth a few risks.

But a Texas Ranger named Leander McNelly did everything he could to make it a more risky business. One historian described him as a "tallish man of quiet manner, with the soft voice of a Methodist minister." One of his men described his method of operation in quite different terms: "If the Mexican proved to be a bandit, we would take charge of him and march him along until we saw a suitable tree .... We'd put a rope over his neck, throw it over a limb and pull him up and down until he consented to tell all he knew. As far as we knew, this treatment always brought out the truth."

On one occasion, after having found out about a bandit drive of stolen cattle, McNelly and his men caught up with them on the open plain. The rustlers thought they were being attacked by soldiers and stood to fight. Had they known this was a force of Texas Rangers, they'd have turned and run. Which they soon did.

The Rangers ran after them, and by the time McNelly caught up with the man he was chasing, he had just one shot left in his gun. It was one more than the bandit had, by the way. Rather than following him into the bush, McNelly got off his horse and called to his men that he was out of bullets. That must have amused the Mexican because he came charging out with the biggest grin McNelly had ever seen. And a shiny knife between his teeth. It made a wonderful target for McNelly's last bullet, and he didn't miss.

He lost one of his own men in the fight. The Mexicans lost a dozen. He had their bodies rounded up and carried to the nearest town where they were dumped into a common grave with lots of show, but little ceremony. It was, said McNelly, fair warning to all bandits not to cross to the Texas side, adding that he would "naturalize" them in the same way if they did.

The first Anglo-American woman in Texas, according to tradition, was Jane Wilkinson Long, wife of Dr. James Long, who had been delegated to invade Texas and establish it as a republic after the American Government abandoned Texas in a deal to get Florida from Spain in 1819. They landed at Nacogdoches with a force of 300 volunteers. They took it easily, and Long went off to Galveston to get some help from Jean Lafitte, the pirate. While he was gone, the Spanish defeated his small army. His wife and child had escaped back into Louisiana and Long rejoined her. But he didn't get over his idea of an independent Texas, and soon they were back attacking the Spanish coast. They established a fort there, and Long went off again, this time to Mexico City, once again leaving Jane and now two children behind.

He was captured by the Mexicans. When word got back to the fort, his supporters went their separate ways, leaving Jane Long alone with her children, a teenage black slave girl named Kian and a dog named Galveston.

They took most of the food, but left them with some fishhooks and an old cannon. They spent the winter alone in the fort, living on oysters and fish and raw courage. Then one day a band of Indians appeared. Jane was certain they'd kill them all, and just as likely eat them. As a last-ditch effort, she hoisted a red petticoat to the top of a flagpole and fired a shot from the cannon. The Indians, thinking they might be the ones to be swallowed alive, turned and ran. During that winter, Jane Long, who was just twenty-one years old at the time, gave birth to her third daughter. The child was fatherless. Jane Long's husband had been shot by the Mexicans. "An accident," they said.

Then one morning as spring was coming on, Jane saw a ship passing. She hailed it and it came to her rescue. It contained the first colonists on their way to Stephen Austin's new colony.

When she discovered that her husband had been killed, she rode hundreds of miles into Mexico to have his killer punished. When she realized it was a fool's errand, she turned around and went back home to Mississippi. But the lure of Texas, even then, was too strong. A few years later, she went back and settled down there. A very much honored woman in her own time.

It isn't known why Jane Long had chosen to scare off the Indians with a flannel petticoat. She had a perfectly good flag that she and her sister had designed and sewn. It was made of white silk with a red stripe and red fringe all around. And on a red ground in the upper corner, it had a white star.

A lone star.

From the streets of Laredo to the Red River Valley; from the citrus groves of the Rio Grande Valley to the Latin flavor of El Paso, from the grasslands of the Panhandle to the wide open spaces of West Texas, there isn't a single word that can describe all of Texas. Except that is, the original word itself, *Teychas*. Friend.

Of all the words people associate with Texas, the ones you hear most often are probably "oil" or "millionaire," "wide open spaces" or "cowboy." It's a fact Texas produces more oil than any other state. But it's also a fact, Texas ranks tenth among the states in the number of millionaires. As for wide open spaces, there's still plenty of that, but a lot of Texans never go outdoors at all except for an occasional bicycle ride or at vacation time. Cowboys? Well, Texas still has its share, but there are probably more working cowboys up in Montana and Wyoming. Of course, everything they know was taught to them either directly or indirectly by Texans. But as any rodeo fan will tell you, the state of the art has moved on.

Rodeos were once the prime form of entertainment in Texas. They began as an extension of the work-day on the ranch, but with the added excitement of competition to see who was best at roping and tying, riding and breaking wild horses, bulldogging steers. Texas cowboys, by tradition, were always the best in the world when it came to handling a lariat. But today, the great ropers seem to have gone. They've been replaced by bull riders, mainly, and that's the big event at Texan rodeos today. You don't have to be a cowboy to be a bull rider, you see. It's the one rodeo event that has absolutely nothing to do with the cowboy's working world. You don't even have to know how to ride a horse to ride a bull. All you need is guts. It's a perfect event for city boys who like to keep in touch with the Old West; and since their country cousins don't get any more chance than they do to practice the sport, everybody is on more or less equal footing.

But football has long since replaced rodeo as the number one sport in Texas. In fact, the National Finals Rodeo, the World Series of roping and riding, takes place every year in Oklahoma. And Texans don't win nearly as often as they did a generation ago.

It's what happens when you get "citified."

In the big cities and small towns of Texas, they hang on to their rural roots with a passion for country music. Almost every town has a honky-tonk bar where you can eat peanuts from a big barrel, drink beer from a long-neck bottle and do the two-step to the songs of people like Hank Williams or Eddie Rabbit.

Lately, some discos have found their way into Dallas and Houston, but flashing lights and monotonous thumping from expensive sound systems doesn't quite fit the Texas mood. Besides, you can't go to a disco in pipestem jeans and a checkered shirt. So Texans did what Texans often do, they adapted the fad to suit them rather than the other way around as happens in the other forty-nine states.

The result is that country discos are cropping up all over Texas. They have some of the character of the old honky-tonks; the 'cor with stuffed deer heads and branding irons randomly hung on the walls. But they don't have as many fist fights, and the sound equipment is much too expensive to let anyone throw a beer bottle at anyone else. They have the flashing lights of a standard disco, and they have disc jockeys who make sure the music never stops. But the music is different and so are the customers. Both are Texan to the core.

Merle Haggard, Leon Russell, Chet Atkins and all the other big country music stars sell a lot of records in Texas. But the biggest of them all is a Texan named Willie Nelson, who along with people like Waylon Jennings, did a very typically Texan thing to the pop record industry.

By tradition, the big decisions about who records what in the country music field are made in Nashville, Tennessee. And since so many Texans have roots in Tennessee, that should be all right by them. But Texans don't much like following anybody. And Willie Nelson is a Texan. So much so, that many Texans will tell you that if you don't understand Willie, you don't understand Texas. He developed a style that fits the country mood, but adds a Texas flavor. It brings Nashville in line with present-day America and at the same time takes country music back to its basics. Where an ordinary country singer might moan about having tears in his ears from lying in bed crying over a lost love, the Texas version would add a stanza saying that it's OK because any time now he'll find someone to blow in his ear and dry up those tears.

Hope is what makes the difference. And hope always has been important to Texans. Life never was easy in that tough land, but they always knew it would get better. They never were very good at wringing their hands. And, while their past has always given them plenty to talk about, the future is what counts most.

And the future of Texas has never looked better.

The Lone Star Flag (previous page) flutters a welcome to the state named from a Caddo Indian word taysa, *meaning "friends." The state flag was originally the flag of the independent Republic of Texas from 1836-1845. In downtown Dallas (overleaf), the fifty-story Reunion Tower (right) — topped by a geodesic dome containing a revolving restaurant, forms the focal point of the Reunion area, which was once a nineteenth-century settlement of French immigrants. Beside it stands the black and gleaming Hyatt Regency Hotel, and nearby is white Union Station and the gray-roofed, red limestone building of the Old County Courthouse.*

35

Eighty-foot-high flagpoles appear to pierce the steps outside Dallas City Hall (right), which was designed by the famous architect I.M. Pei. The InterFirst Plaza in downtown Dallas (overleaf) towers tall against the center of the skyline.

Aldredge House (these pages), built in 1916, is located on Swiss Avenue in Dallas and is part of the Swiss Avenue Historic Association. Its interior walls are lined with a light mahogany, which is perfectly complemented by the dusty-rose-colored stair carpet (facing page bottom). Swiss Avenue is the site of many sumptuous houses of varying styles, ranging from Jacobean and Elizabethan Revival, Prairie Style and Neo Classical to late twentieth-century. Overleaf: the Lincoln Hotel, now the Doubletree Hotel, Dallas.

Right: Main Street, Fort Worth (overleaf), seen from outside the Tarrant County Convention Center. The Center covers a notorious area known as Hell's Half Acre until its destruction at the time of World War I. Many famous criminals spent time there: Butch Cassidy and the Sundance Kid, "The Hole in the Wall Gang" and, later, Bonnie and Clyde. Fort Worth began life as an isolated military post in 1849 and, being a convenient stopping-off point along the Chisholm Trail, the town was frequently full of rowdy cowboys.

Main Street on a night before Christmas, when avenues of trees glow with festive lights, seems a picture of quiet civilization, and it is difficult to imagine Fort Worth's riotous, Wild-West past. Today's rangers, cowboys and gamblers are most likely to be baseball players, footballers and stockbrokers.

Old Fort Parker State Historic Site (these pages), near Groesbeck, is the site of the fort built in 1834 by John Parker. In 1836, it was attacked by Comanches and several of the Parker family were killed. Five of them were captured, among them nine-year-old Cynthia Ann, who was eventually to marry the Commanche Chief Peta Nacona and take the name Neduah. She and one of her children were captured in 1860 while they tried to escape from Captain Sul Ross' attack on the Nawkohnees' camp. Ross noticed Neduah's blue eyes, realized that she was not an Indian and returned her to her Texan relatives. In October, 1864, she died, it is said of a broken heart, longing to return to the free ways of the Comanches. She was only thirty-seven years old.

Long, pale shafts of cypress trees, hung with Spanish moss, rise out of the waters of Lake Caddo, in Caddo Lake State Park, near Jefferson. The Caddo Indians believed that the lake had been created by the Great Spirit. According to their legend, a chief was warned in a dream to move his people to higher ground before an onslaught of heavy rains. No sooner had he done so than the earth shuddered, sundered and water rushed up through the split ground to form a lake. The more often cited cause for Lake Caddo's formation is that it was formed by the Great Raft, a series of natural log jams which blocked the Red River, causing the water to build up in its tributaries.

The House of the Seasons (above), in Jefferson, was built in 1872 by Benjamin H. Epperson, a prominent lawyer, entrepreneur, political leader and a friend of Sam Houston. The house is named for its cupola, each wall of which is set with a different color of stained glass, evoking a season of the year. Top right: the master bedroom and (right) the hall with its small, railed atrium, through which visitors looking up can see inside the cupola.

Right and overleaf: downtown Houston. This city was the creation of two New York real estate promoters, J.K. and A.C. Allen, who were looking for a place to build "a great center of government and commerce." Accordingly, in August 1836, they bought 6,642 acres of land from Mrs. T.F.L. Parrott, the widow of John Austin, for $9,428. The brothers decided to call the city after their hero, Sam Houston, hoping that with such a suitable site and name, their city would be selected as the capital of Texas. It seemed to the Allen brothers that "Nature seems to have designated this place for the future seat of government," and they described the city itself as "handsome and beautifully elevated, salubrious and well-watered, and now in the very heart and center of population." All of which is as true of Houston today.

Top: the Sheraton-Houston Hotel with the pink InterFirst Plaza to the left and, behind it, the curved Allied Bank Building. Twenty-one miles southeast of downtown Houston, the 570-foot-high San Jacinto Monument (above) commemorates Sam Houston's decisive victory over Santa Anna, won with the stirring cry, "Remember the Alamo!" Facing page: the Wortham Fountains in Tranquility Park, and (overleaf) the bandstand and St. John Church in Sam Houston Park, all in Houston.

The red roof of Marriott's Hotel stands out behind the piers of Galveston's Seawall Boulevard.

Italianate Ashton Villa (these pages) was built in 1859 for James Moreau Brown, and survived the onslaughts of history and climate. It came through the 1900 hurricane relatively undamaged to become the showpiece of the Galveston Historical Society as the town's oldest restored building. The Society has preserved Ashton Villa in its nineteenth-century state with as many of the family artifacts and possessions as possible in situ. Accordingly, the house gives a fascinating glimpse into the lives, for example, of the powerful Colonel Brown and the eccentric traveler, Miss Bettie Brown. The dining room (top left) has been arranged in accordance wih the details of a photograph, taken in 1913, of the table set for a bridal party. The room was extended during the 1870s, enabling the family to accommodate forty guests at their table. The matching sideboard and window cornices date from this refurbishment. The Gold Room (left) served as the formal entertaining room for the Browns. The pier mirrors, window cornices and the chandelier are all original to the room, and some of the large paintings hanging on the walls are the work of Miss Bettie Brown. The original parlor piano was one item of furniture which could not be saved during the 1900 storm, which flooded the first floor. It was too heavy to be carried to the second floor, and floated out of the house, eventually to be used as a raft by a Galvestonian who survived to tell the tale.

The Ionic columns which decorate the First
Methodist Church on Lavaca Street lend it an
Ancient-World grandeur with which it does not
appear out of place before the Texas State
Capitol, Austin. The city was named to honor
Stephen F. Foster, father of the Republic, of
whom Mary Austin Holley, writing in 1836,
said: "It is uncertain how long this extensive and
valuable country would have remained unknown
and unsettled, had not the bold enterprise and
perseverance of the Austins torn away the veil
that hid it from view of the world, and redeemed
it from the wilderness, by the settlement of a
flourishing colony of North Americans, on the
Brazos and Colorado Rivers."

Above: the Senate Chamber of the 1888 Capitol Building (these pages) in Austin. The bronze monument (facing page) dedicated to Terry's Texas Rangers was sculpted by Pompeo Coppini and mounted in 1907 to commemorate the Texas Rangers who served the Confederacy during the Civil War. The Capitol's cornerstone was laid on the 49th anniversary of the Battle of San Jacinto, March 2, 1885, to a 49-gun salute. The Governor, John Ireland, then asked the assembled crowd to confirm: "Which is better? Limestone or granite?" they cried: "Red granite!" – the material chosen for civic buildings ever since.

The Governor's Mansion (these pages), located at 11th and Colorado, was built in 1856 by Abner Cook in the Greek Revival style and stands within the Capitol complex in Austin. The Governor and his family live in a small, private apartment within the building; the rest of the house is open to the public. Above: the hall, and (facing page) the Conservatory both with unusual carpets.

Right: Austin seen across Town Lake. Behind the Littlefield Fountain (top right) the Main Building and floodlit Texas Tower of the University of Texas, Austin, are seen silhouetted against the evening sky. The Lyndon Baines Johnson Presidential Library and Museum (above) stands on the University of Texas campus. The Library was established by L.B. Johnson after he left office, and the Museum contains general and biographical presidential exhibits, including a replica of the Oval Office.

Top left: the reconstructed Lyndon B. Johnson Birthplace on the L.B. Johnson Ranch. Johnson had said of his home "It is impossible to live on this land without being a part of it," and he frequently returned to the ranch to relax while in office. The Ranch House (above), known as the "Texas White House," used to belong to his Uncle Clarence and Aunt Frank Martin but, by 1951, the widowed Aunt Frank could not cope with the upkeep and the Johnsons bought the deteriorating house from her, with some trepidation on Lady Bird's part. Johnson's boyhood home (left) from 1913, in Johnson City, is now part of the L.B. Johnson National Historical Park (these pages).

Above: the parlor of the Lyndon B. Johnson Birthplace, where the President was born on August 27, 1908. Johnson's earliest memory was of this place on a dark night: his father was away and his lonely mother was drawing water outside, weeping. "I'll take care of you, Mama," said Lyndon. Top: the Ranch House's living room. Facing page: (top) the East Bedrooom of the Birthplace, and (bottom) the den of the Ranch House.

Enchanted Rock State Natural Area contains a
variety of pink granite outcrops, all part of the
huge Enchanted Rock batholith, or inselberg –
island mountain – which has been exposed
through millions of years of erosion. It is one of
the oldest exposed rocks in North America and a
well-known feature of the Central Mineral
Region of Texas. The rock itself is said to be over
a billion years old. Local Indians revered it,
fearing that it contained evil spirits – possibly
because it appears to glitter on moonlit nights
after rain, and emit strange creaking noises of
contraction on cool nights following hot days.

It is difficult to believe that the landscaped River Walk (these pages) along the San Antonio River might never have come into existence. In the 1930s there were plans afoot to cover over the river and use it as a sewer. Fortunately, it was saved, and the walk along its banks now offers a peaceful retreat to the citizens of San Antonio. Overleaf: HemisFair Plaza, San Antonio, the site, in 1968, of San Antonio's World Fair, which marked the city's 250th anniversary.

Top left: InterFirst Bank on East Martin Street, San Antonio (these pages), and (left) East Houston Street Bridge over the San Antonio River. Above: downtown San Antonio, seen from the observation level of the Tower of the Americas, and (overleaf) the facade of the Alamo chapel. During a lull in the bombardment of Alamo by the Mexican General Santa Anna, Colonel William Travis unsheathed his sword and traced a line in the dust. The situation was hopeless and all he could say to his men was "those prepared to give their lives in freedom's cause, come over to me." All 188 men crossed the line, except James Bowie, stricken with typhoid-pneumonia, who asked that he be carried over. They all died. Bowie, his knife bloodied, his pistols empty and his body riddled with bullets, died on his cot. Sam Houston wrote of the battle to General Santa Anna in these terms: "humanity itself would blush to class you among the chivalric spirits of the age of vandalism …. So far as I was concerned in preserving your life and subsequent liberation, I was only influenced by considerations of mercy, humanity, and the establishment of a national character." The spirit of the Alamo has indeed become part of the character of Texas.

These pages: the Corpus Christi Marina, enclosed within a protective breakwater. The Port of Corpus Christi was established in 1926 and is authorized to harbor vessels up to forty-five feet in depth – the deepest port on the Gulf coast, which means that it handles a wide range of ships from different countries.

Fulton Mansion, in Fulton, was built by Colonel George Ware Fulton – a cattle baron – and completed in 1876. Its guest list included such names as General Robert E. Lee and Jefferson Davis. The Rio Grande flows through Big Bend National Park before meeting the waters of Lake Amistad (overleaf). This lovely land lives up to the words of Mary Austin Holley spoken in 1836: "Quite unexpectedly, a report has reached the public ear that the country lying west of the Sabine River is a tract of surpassing beauty, exceeding even our best western lands in productiveness, with a climate perfectly salubrious, and of a temperature, at all seasons of the year, most delightful."

Left: the weathered peaks of Panther Pass, Big Bend National Park, and (overleaf) yuccas growing at Sotol Vista Overlook give Texas an atmosphere of unconquered wilderness even today.

Above: the rocky valley of the Rio Grande (right) between Redford and Lajitas, marking the border with Mexico. The Texan naturalist, Roy Bedichek, describing the road that traces the Rio Grande at the edge of the desiccated foothills, comments on the "river verdure which serves to underscore the desert and make the traveler more fully conscious of it." Overleaf: Pulliam Ridge in Big Bend National Park.

Facing page and top: the church of the 1681 Nuestra Senora de la Concepcion del Socorro Mission, near El Paso. The Nuestra Señora del Carmen (above) was established in 1682 outside El Paso to minister to the Tigua Indians, and it was called Corpus Christi de la Isleta. Now it is known as Ysleta Mission, and is the site of the oldest town in Texas.

Above: El Paso (these pages and overleaf), seen from Tom Lea Park, and (top right) the Civic Center. Right: Kansas Street in downtown El Paso. El Paso city began to spring up on its present site in 1827, below a narrow pass at the foot of Mount Franklin but, ever since Juan de Oñate claimed El Paso del Rio Grande del Norte for Spain in 1598, the city's spirit has been Hispanic. Being isolated from the distant events of the Texas Revolution, El Paso shared a common religion, language and history with the Mexican town of Juárez. There is still a sense of the old town and how it was in 1895. At that time, gunman John Wesley Hardin was shot dead in the Acme Saloon. He had actually been pardoned, become a reformed man and, ironically enough, a practicing lawyer, when a local constable shot him dead. For many years after Hardin's death, El Paso was a convenient place for outlaws to cross the Rio Grande.

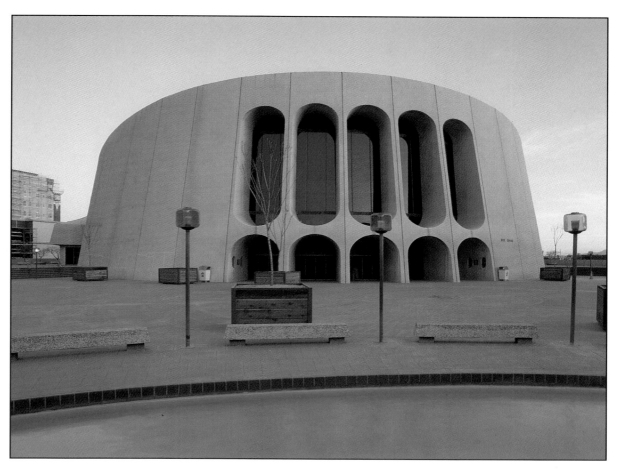

The Magoffin Home (these pages), completed by 1875 for Joseph Magoffin, was built in El Paso of sun-dried adobe and decorated with Greek Revival details, in the form of pedimented doors and windows (top). Above and facing page bottom: the parlor, and (facing page top) the family parlor.

The barren peak of El Capitan (right) in Guadalupe Mountains National Park was once the thriving Capitan reef, formed up to 280 million years ago principally by lime-secreting algae. These days, it is very difficult to imagine the arid Guadalupe Mountains (overleaf) ever being under water.

The desolate dunes of Monahans Sandhills State Park, southwest of Odessa, pocked with transient footprints. Overleaf: downtown Lubbock, home of the Texas Tech University.

The Amarillo Livestock Auctions (these pages) are held at the Western Stockyards in Amarillo every week and are the center of trade for the immense ranching lands of the Texas Panhandle.

The Lighthouse Peak in the Palo Duro Canyon is probably one of the best-known landmarks of Palo Duro Canyon State Park. It is a pillar of soft mudstone, about seventy-five feet high, capped with a layer of sandstone. The name palo duro comes from the Spanish for "hard wood," and refers to the juniper that grows along the rim of the canyon. Overleaf: the view west from the scenic overlook of Timber Creek Canyon. Following page: the Prairie Dog Town Fork of the Red River.